Smoke and Flames

Story by Tim Harris

Illustrations by Ash Roy

Smoke and Flames

Text: Tim Harris
Publishers: Tania Mazzeo and Eliza Webb
Series consultant: Amanda Sutera
Hands on Heads Consulting
Editor: Sarah Layton
Project editor: Annabel Smith
Designer: Jess Kelly
Project designer: Danielle Maccarone
Illustrations: Ash Roy
Production controller: Renee Tome

NovaStar

ISBN 978 0 17 033468 6

Cengage Learning Australia
Level 5, 80 Dorcas Street
Southbank VIC 3006 Australia
Phone: 1300 790 853
Email: aust.nelsonprimary@cengage.com

For learning solutions, visit **cengage.com.au**

Printed in China by 1010 Printing International Ltd
1 2 3 4 5 6 7 29 28 27 26 25

Nelson acknowledges the Traditional Owners and Custodians of the lands of all First Nations Peoples. We pay respect to Elders past and present, and extend that respect to all First Nations Peoples today.

Contents

Chapter 1

Smoke

Lawson didn't notice how thick the smoke had become outside. If he had looked up from his phone, he might have seen the blanket of white begin to wrap tightly around the house.

The smoke had been around for days. Its ashy-eucalypt scent had seeped under the door frames on Christmas Eve. But today, the smoke was getting worse.

Lawson, however, was only concerned about one thing: mastering one of the games on his new phone. The phone had been a Christmas present from his mum. Although she had been hesitant to give him one in the first place, she had eventually agreed.

"You're growing up so quickly," Mum had told Lawson on Christmas Day. "So I thought it was time you had your own phone. Plus, we're a long way out of town, and I ... well, I just want you to be prepared."

Lawson's mum was always going on about the importance of being prepared, especially during bushfire season. She was part of the Rural Fire Service, so it was her job to think about fire plans. Today, she was fighting a large fire about 15 kilometres out of town.

When Lawson eventually looked up from his phone and saw how thick the smoke had become, his heartbeat quickened. "What's going on out there?" he said to himself. He closed the game and checked for messages. There was a new one from his mother.

Hi Lawson,

The winds have picked up today. Remember the plan and keep checking the app for updates. I'll keep in touch when I can. Duncan knows to take you into town if you need to evacuate.

Love Mum

The plan. At least his mother had everything under control. She had printed out the plan and stuck it to the fridge. Lawson headed to the kitchen to read it again.

Family Fire Plan

If I'm out fighting fires, follow these steps:

1 *Keep an eye on the bushfire app and/or check in with me.*
2 *If a warning is sent out, call Grandpa and make sure he knows to evacuate.*
3 *Get a lift into town with Duncan from next door (don't wait for me!).*
4 *Take the box near the front door with you (it has our important documents inside).*
5 *Text or call me to let me know that you are safe.*

"I should check the bushfire app," Lawson reminded himself.

Lawson headed back to the lounge room and snatched up his phone from the couch. To his shock, the battery had drained to just one per cent. He hadn't been paying attention to it when he was playing the game.

Lawson fetched his charger and hastily plugged it into a power point. But then, without warning, the air conditioner cut out and the television – which had been silently showing cartoons in the background – turned off. No power. There must be a blackout.

Lawson opened the bushfire app and briefly caught a glimpse of a bright-red WARNING icon. But just as quickly, it disappeared as the screen went dead – the battery was out!

I should have checked the app earlier, thought Lawson, now frustrated with himself.

Lawson raced to the house phone to call Mum. He sighed with relief when he heard the dial tone sound, which meant the phone was still working despite the power outage. But when Mum didn't pick up, his throat turned dry. Was she too busy fighting the fires to answer? Was she okay?

He tried calling Grandpa next. To his dismay, there was no answer on the other end. He wished Grandpa had agreed to get a mobile phone at Christmas, too, but the old man had been content with his house phone.

Lawson was now both scared and angry with himself. Why hadn't he been paying attention earlier? Why hadn't he thought to keep up with the latest bushfire updates?

Suddenly, a loud siren pierced the air outside.

Chapter 2

Evacuation

The siren was coming from the end of the street. It was a police car. The officer driving the vehicle was shadowing a pair of constables who were dashing between houses. Lawson could hear one of the constables, who was now just a few doors down.

"Sorry, ma'am, there is no time for that. You need to get into your car and drive to the evacuation centre immediately."

Lawson grabbed the box of important documents near the front door and stepped outside. He could see his neighbour Duncan loading plastic tubs into the back of his beaten-up station wagon. Duncan locked eyes with Lawson, then gave a nod when he spotted the box under Lawson's arm. "Good job, mate. I was just about to come and get you."

"Have you heard from my mum?" asked Lawson.

Duncan shook his head. "No. But I've been keeping an eye on the news and the bushfire app." He went on. "The wind has turned, and the fire is now heading directly towards us. It's terrifying how quickly the conditions can change!"

Lawson could feel the hot breeze blowing in from the west. It was pressing his t-shirt against his chest, dusting the black cotton with tiny pieces of ash. He also noticed that he couldn't even see the sun because the smoke was so thick.

"Everything will be okay," said Duncan. He must have read the worry on Lawson's face. "Your mum will have all the latest information, and her team will be on top of things."

Lawson desperately wanted to ask Duncan about Grandpa, but he could sense Duncan was in a rush.

"I should have been paying more attention," Lawson muttered to himself. He frowned at his uncharged phone, which he had added to the box before taking it from the front door.

The young constable who was working on Lawson's side of the street reached the driveway and glanced around the outside of the house. "Is there anyone else inside, young man?" she asked.

"No, it's just me. I've arranged to go to the evacuation centre with my neighbour." Lawson pointed towards Duncan. "Mum is out fighting the fires."

"Well done," said the constable. "I'm glad you have a plan." She nodded at Lawson and turned towards the next house, on a mission to clear the street as quickly as possible.

"What about my grandpa?" Lawson called after the constable.

She quickly spun around. "Where is he?"

"He lives out on Western Ridge Road."

The young constable frowned momentarily. "We couldn't access that area because the flames had already reached it. The fire crew told us to start the evacuation here. But I'm sure he's okay ..." With that, she dashed to the next house to continue clearing the residents.

Lawson wasn't so sure. Was Grandpa okay? Did he evacuate in time?

Panicked, he slipped into the passenger side of Duncan's car and shakily fastened the seat belt. He would try to call Grandpa again when he got to the evacuation centre. For now, he would have to hold Duncan's pet guinea pig until they reached town.

Duncan turned the key in the ignition, and the radio buzzed to life in sync with the car's engine. A newsreader was part-way through a bushfire update.

"... three houses have been destroyed just kilometres west of town. Residents in surrounding areas are advised to evacuate immediately. Firefighters face an uphill battle, but extra crew are arriving from the city to lend a hand."

Somewhere overhead, a helicopter whooshed past as it headed west.

Chapter 3

Coming Together

The community hall made for the perfect evacuation centre. It was located at the mouth of the river and, with a golf course separating it from the scrubland on the other side, it was well-positioned to shelter evacuees from any threat of fire. The Rural Fire Service kept the hall well-stocked with water and first-aid equipment during bushfire season.

Lawson thanked Duncan for driving him and carried his box inside the hall.

Despite the blackout, the hall was a hive of activity. It was packed with newly arrived locals, most looking both relieved and worried. Some were cradling their pets and hugging loved ones. An elderly lady sat in one corner, fanning herself with an old magazine.

Lawson immediately spotted Jenny, his mum's best friend. She also worked with the Rural Fire Service, and her cheeks were blackened with soot. She must have been on a break.

Lawson retrieved a notebook with Grandpa's phone number in it from the box. He plonked the box on an empty plastic seat and skidded straight up to Jenny. "Is Mum okay?"

Jenny nodded. “Your mum is fine. You know what she’s like – never one to back down from a challenge. She’s with the crew to the north. A separate blaze started there a couple of hours ago. I just got back from the west. It’s a lot worse there, and –”

“Did you see Grandpa?”

A deep crease appeared in Jenny’s brow. “Your mum told me that you were in charge of checking on Grandpa.”

Lawson looked down at his sneakers. “I got distracted ...”

"Let me try calling him. Is his number written in here?" There was worry in Jenny's voice. She took the notebook from Lawson and punched a number into her phone.

Lawson's heart froze when he heard a recorded voice from the telephone company crackle on the other end of the line. "The number you have called is not connected ..."

This was turning into a nightmare! Why was Grandpa's line disconnected? Lawson couldn't even bring himself to consider the possibilities.

To make matters worse, a tall man in a firefighting uniform approached Jenny and spoke to her hurriedly. “We need to leave now. Another house has been lost on Western Ridge Road.” There was a sense of urgency in the man’s voice – an energy that added a horrifying weight to his words.

“Grandpa,” Lawson whispered to himself.

He didn’t notice when Jenny put a cold bottle of water in his hands. He didn’t notice when she squeezed him goodbye. He didn’t notice when she told him that she would get word to him when she heard anything.

He was too numb.

Chapter 4

Flames

"Are you okay?"

It took Lawson a moment to realise the voice was speaking to him.

A young man was sitting on the chair next to Lawson. He was cradling a blue-tongued lizard in his arms. The lizard's brightly coloured tongue flicked the air, as if testing to see if Lawson was a threat.

"Are you okay?" repeated the man.

Lawson sighed. "I don't know. I can't get hold of my grandpa. His house phone is disconnected. He lives out on Western Ridge Road."

"Sometimes house phones can be disrupted in situations like this," said the young man. He placed the lizard on his shoulder and retrieved a mobile phone from his pocket. "I kept this fully charged. I can still get some news coverage despite the blackout."

Lawson watched with wide eyes as the young man tuned in to a news report. Helicopter footage showed a fire tearing through bushland. The camera panned to the side, highlighting a row of burning houses with cars ablaze in the driveways.

"That's Grandpa's house!" Lawson pointed to a small cottage with a bright-blue roof – incredibly, it was untouched by the flames.

The young man shook his head in disbelief. "Looks like the choppers have managed to save a few homes in that street."

"I hope Grandpa is okay …" managed Lawson.

“Is someone looking for me?” A familiar voice spoke suddenly from behind Lawson, and a strong hand squeezed his shoulder.

Lawson spun around to see Grandpa smiling down at him. “The fire service got us out just in time – they always have a plan, just like that mother of yours.”

Lawson leapt to his feet and hugged his grandpa like he hadn’t seen him in years.

Chapter 5

Rebuilding

The late March rains added heavy humidity to the air. It was now three months since the fires, and Lawson was amazed to see several bright-green bursts of regrowth scattered across the trunks of blackened trees. The plants that lined the road all seemed to have gained new life, and Western Ridge Road was filled with the same vibrant energy.

"The bush always bounces back," said Grandpa, admiring the sprouts of new green leaves. "Just like the people do."

The local community had set up a team to help rebuild many of the homes affected by the Christmas fires. Lawson had volunteered to chip in as soon as he heard about the project, and he was working to clear leaves from the new foundation of one of the homes while Grandpa watched on.

"I'm glad you got out in time, Grandpa," said Lawson, sweeping a particularly stubborn leaf off the edge of the concrete.

"Me too, Lawson. If it wasn't for our firefighters and your mother's plan ..."

Lawson's mother was out of town filming a community-service advertisement about bushfire plans. She was the perfect choice for the role. Lawson couldn't wait for the advertisement to show on television and social media.

Grandpa surveyed his street and sighed. "That was the closest call I've ever had with a fire. They'll be busy with hazard reduction burning in the coming years to try and prevent this from happening again."

Lawson allowed himself to smile. With so many people lending a hand, the affected homes on Western Ridge Road would be rebuilt in no time. And most of all, he was glad that nobody was hurt.

"Come on, Grandpa, let's get the leaves off this section." Lawson held out a broom. "Grandpa?"

But Grandpa didn't respond straight away. He had taken his brand-new mobile phone out of his pocket and was distracted by a game. "Sure, Lawson, I've just got to clear this level ..."

Lawson shook his head and got to work. "And I thought I was bad ..."